VENTRILOQUISM

VENTRILOQUISM

By

HAROLD G. KING

AND

JUGGLING

By

JOHN E. T. CLARK

London

C. Arthur Pearson, Ltd

Henrietta Street, W.C.

1921

Printing Statement:

Due to the very old age and scarcity of this book, many of the pages may be hard to read due to the blurring of the original text, possible missing pages, missing text and other issues beyond our control.

Because this is such an important and rare work, we believe it is best to reproduce this book regardless of its original condition.

Thank you for your understanding.

CONTENTS

9

INTRODUCTION TO VENTRILOQUISM

I HAVE always been surprised that so many people imagine a ventriloquist must be "born and not made." It is generally believed that unless a person has certain gifts from birth it is impossible to acquire the fascinating art of ventriloquism. This is entirely wrong. Any aspirant whose vocal organs are in a normal condition can become a ventriloquist without any undue exertion. Of course, practice is necessary, for practice spells efficiency in all things.

Broadly speaking, let me summarise under the following headings just what a ventriloquist must be able to do :

1. He must have the ability to create a ventriloquial voice without any perceptible movement of his lips.

2. He must be able to manipulate a ventriloquial figure.

3. He must have good dialogue to introduce into his entertainment.

Now a few minutes' consideration is sufficient to prove that items two and three form no real obstacle in the path of the beginner. As to item one, adequate study of the tables of practice to be found herein forms the backbone of the ventriloquial art.

So do not commence a study of ventriloquism with the firm idea that the almost impossible is being attempted.

The various articles and tables of practice have been set in sequence, so that the reader may proceed step by step until proficient. Each table covers the articles which precede it, thus forming a complete lesson in every case. I realise that some of the exercises will appear superfluous, even almost absurd, to the beginner, but I ask for their full acceptance, because they are the result of experimenting over many years of practical ventriloquism.

I have attempted to write the book in simple language, eliminating any literary style. May this serve as an apology for any errors discovered herein.

VENTRILOQUISM

THE VENTRILOQUIAL VOICE

To acquire a ventriloquial voice the performer must primarily master the art of creating an entirely different voice from his natural speech, and then produce that voice clearly, without any perceptible movement of the mouth. Naturally, the tone of a ventriloquial voice will depend on the kind of figure the ventriloquist uses. It is useless to produce a gruff voice for a doll dressed as an Eton boy, or a falsetto voice for a coster figure. Therefore the voice has to be adapted to suit the doll. Broadly speaking, the following details should be sufficient for the beginner to understand the voice required for various kinds of ventriloquial figures :

ETON BOY	. A refined and high-pitched voice.
COSTER .	. A lower - pitched voice, sharp, ungrammatical and with a suspicion of nasal.
OLD MAN	. A low drawn - out and slightly gruff voice.

PAGE BOY . A moderately high-pitched and cheeky voice.

SOLDIER . . A moderately low-pitched and ungrammatical voice.

GIRL . . A falsetto voice, produced with slowness and more refined.

SERVANT GIRL . A falsetto voice, but coarser and ungrammatical.

The important thing to aim at is the production of a ventriloquial voice as strikingly different as possible from the natural voice.

Next comes the question of talking without any movement of the lips. At this point let me dispose of the theory that a ventriloquist talks with his lips closed. This is practically impossible, for the lips must be slightly parted to permit the clear passage of speech from the throat. It is the teeth that are closed, but only lightly. A certain amount of control is required to keep the lips immobile during ventriloquial speech and closing the teeth helps this considerably, although it is not absolutely essential.

The beginner will find it quite an easy matter to clearly pronounce certain words without any movement of the lips. As a comparative test, close the teeth lightly and with lips parted, but immobile, say, " How are you ? " Similarly try to say " Better purchase the butter," and it will be found impossible to pronounce this sentence with phonetic clearness unless the lips are allowed to meet as each word is spoken.

So there are certain letters or sounds which are obstacles in the way of clear ventriloquial speech and they are the five following letters of the alphabet, " b," " m," " p," " v," and " w." The other twenty-one letters can be pronounced clearly and with ease, as little practice will prove. Now there are two ways of surmounting this difficulty. Some performers allow their lips to close when pronouncing a difficult word. This certainly gives clearness of speech, but at the same time considerably lessens the effect of good ventriloquial voice production. The alternative is to keep the lips still and pronounce the nearest sound to the actual phonetic sound of such words. This is by far the better method of the two, because the slight difference in pronunciation passes almost unnoticed by the audience and the performer enjoys the distinction of creating a ventriloquial voice without the least sign of any lip movement. I shall take it for granted that my readers have chosen this method.

Strictly speaking, therefore, the sound of the alphabet spoken ventriloquially is as follows : a, " ge," c, d, e, f, g, h, i, j, k, l, " emg," n, o, " ke," q, r, s, t, u, " wve," " dugglew," x, y, z.

Having mastered the art of speaking the alphabet thus, the beginner will find himself talking in short sentences with a ventriloquial voice (see first Table of Practice).

Next a study of facial expression becomes necessary. The ventriloquial voice must not appear to concern the performer at all. It is the " voice " of a doll seated on the performer's knee, or an imaginary person behind a screen, in a box, under the floor or elsewhere, so the face of the performer must essentially be natural the whole time he is producing ventriloquial speech or sound.

Even after one has completely mastered the art of talking with immobile lips, it will be found that the forehead has a tendency to move in harmony, so to speak, with the ventriloquial sound produced. Here again, control is needed, combined with practice before a mirror.

The whole thing amounts to this. The performer must produce a ventriloquial voice whilst outwardly appearing unconscious of the fact. Therein lies the perfect illusion.

TABLE OF PRACTICE

FIRST STAGE

VOICE PRODUCTION

(THIS book contains five Tables of Practice, each of which should be carefully studied until the beginner is sufficiently proficient to proceed to the next stage.)

1. Deliver the alphabet with the teeth lightly closed and attempt to keep the lips immobile. Special attention must be given to sounding the letters " b," " m," " p," " v," and " w," as explained in the previous article.

Continue this practice until thoroughly proficient in clear pronunciation. Carry out the exercise in front of a mirror, this enabling one to correct any faults in facial expression.

2. Repeat exercise No. 1, but endeavour to create a higher pitched voice. This is the first step towards acquiring a uniform ventriloquial voice (assumed voice).

3. Practise the delivery of short ventriloquial sentences, paying. more attention to perfecting the assumed voice than to the actual words used.

Aim at producing the voice of a Coster or Schoolboy, other voices being developed with further practice.

4. Ask simple questions in an ordinary voice and reply ventriloquially. At the same time study the assumed voice, pronunciation and immobility of lips and face.

The beginner is strongly advised to devote considerable time to the study of this table, before proceeding. Perfection in the above will be the strong foundation of all future work.

THE VENTRILOQUIAL FIGURE

THERE are many kinds of ventriloquial figures, but the type now universally used is what is known as the " Knee figure," popularly called the " Cheeky Boy." The term " knee figure " is used because the doll is a convenient size to carry, and is constructed to sit on the performer's knee (or side of a table). Life-size figures are also used, but naturally these are more bulky and not so easy to manipulate. The most popular characters of the knee figure are such as soldier, sailor, schoolboy, yokel, boy scout, clown, etc.

The head of the figure is supported on a shaft, a wooden rod about nine inches long. The shaft is usually mounted on a semicircular base, which is in turn hinged to the under-part of the figure's neck. To keep the shaft in prolongation with the head, a piece of strong elastic is connected to the side of the base and carried up to a screw concealed under the hair at the back part of the head. So that if the head is pulled forward, the elastic will restore it to an upright position again. By this method the figure can be made to nod.

The shaft fits into the body through an opening

19

which is concealed by the collar of the doll. The body being hollow, the performer can manipulate the shaft from the back through a hole cut in the jacket of the figure.

The mouth movement is worked either by a spring or a pneumatic arrangement, but generally by means of the former. (I do not propose to waste time in giving the details of how a figure works, because the beginner will find this out for himself when he acquires a figure. However, a brief description of the various movements may be useful.)

The movable portion of the mouth is mounted on a bridge, which is pivoted through the centre so as to move up and down. The spring is secured to the head at the top and carried vertically down the inside of the head, the other end being fixed to the bridge. To the under part of the bridge a lead or pull is secured, which passes through a specially constructed passage bored vertically through the neck of the figure. When the head is pulled, the bridge is drawn down, thus causing the mouth to open, and the spring carries same back as soon as the pull is eased.

The end of this pull terminates about half-way down the length of the shaft, the end being attached to a ring or small lever fixed to act on the shaft. It is then an easy matter to hold the shaft with the right hand and at the same time operate the ring or lever with the forefinger, thus combining the head turning and mouth movements. A lever is preferable to a ring, because once the performer looses hold of the latter it is liable to swing and therefore difficult to regain. On the other hand a lever can be released at will and found again at once, being fixed.

The old-fashioned style of mouth movement was very crude. It simply consisted of a movable jaw, which when opened displayed an ugly gap on each side. Many improvements on this have since been made and an up-to-date figure is fitted with a rubber mouth which opens and closes with a perfectly natural effect, being so constructed that the point of the chin does not move at all.

Although I shall always recommend the spring method of opening and closing the mouth, the pneumatic system has certain advantages. For instance, the figure can be controlled without the ventriloquist having his hand inside the body. The mouth is actuated by pressing a bulb, and with the aid of a long length of tubing, this can be done some little distance away from the figure if necessary. Then the bulb can be pressed with the foot leaving both hands free. The deservedly popular ven- triloquist, the Great Coram, concludes his show by bringing " Jerry " to the centre of the stage for a song. This most amusing individual stands by the side of Coram who then works the mouth by a pneumatic arrangement. The bulb is concealed inside the sleeve against " Jerry's " left wrist and it is perfectly natural for Coram to hold the figure's hand and thus control the mouth movement almost unnoticed.

To return to the head of a ventriloquial figure ; this is usually modelled by layers of papier-mâché or pulp and the face painted and finished to the required character. The body can be made of similar material or of box-wood, and the legs and arms padded over a framework of wire or wood. The feet and hands are modelled in wood or plaster, the former, of course, being the most durable material. The clothes are either sewn, gummed, or tacked to the body, and the hair can be real or horse hair.

In addition to the mouth movement, several other effective and amusing mechanical contrivances can be fitted to a figure. I submit a brief description of a variety of these.

SMOKING. The figure is made to smoke by means of a bulb inside the body and a length of thin rubber tubing. This passes through the neck and is connected inside the head to a small piece of iron or brass tubing which is fixed just inside the corner of the mouth. The diameter of this tube must be large enough to hold a cigarette. During the performance the doll asks for a " puff " of the cigarette that the ventriloquist is smoking. The end of the cigarette is then fixed in the tube, and by pressing and releasing the bulb, clouds of smoke are emitted from the mouth of the figure.

MOVING EYES. Each eye is pivoted on a vertical rod, which forms part of a strong wire frame. This frame moves laterally on a bar secured inside the head, a wire spring holding the eyes in their normal place. A lead from the frame runs down through the neck of the figure, terminating at the shaft on a ring or lever, as with the mouth movement. When the lead is pulled the eyes turn slowly on the pivots and the doll appears to be looking out of the corner of its eyes. As the lead is gradually released the spring carries the eyes back to their original position. Many figures are fitted with glass eyes which are very effective.

WINKING EYE. The apparatus for the winking movement might correctly be termed a false eyelid. This is made of thin india-rubber, to one end of which is fixed a half-circle of wire. The ends of this wire are bent outwards to form short flanges which fit into two small holes at each corner of the opening of the eye. The other end of the false eyelid is fixed to the inside of the head, just above the eye, so the rubber forms a blind over the eye, which is kept open by a small spring. By means of the usual lead the eyelid is pulled down and covers the eye, the spring carrying it back again as the cord is slowly released. The effect is a most amusing wink.

MOVABLE WIG. This consists of a strip of hair about two inches in width, running from the centre of the forehead to the back of the head. The strip is firmly mounted on a wire frame so shaped that it will lay naturally over the head and normally appear to be part of the wig. The rear end of the wire frame is bent back to form a short counter-lever and is hinged to the back of the head at the point where it is bent. A cord is fixed to the extreme end of the counter-lever and passed down the collar to a convenient position near the shaft. A short pull will bring the lever down, the counter arrangement causing the movable hair to spring up on the hinge. The weight of the frame will permit the hair to immediately drop back to its original position.

SMILING ACTION. The upper lip is made of india-rubber on a wire mounting. The ends of the wire are pivoted in each corner of the mouth on a similar principle to the winking movement. The lip is held by a small spring and a lead is connected to this and passed down the neck in the usual way. All figures are fitted with a row of teeth (usually made of wood or strong cardboard), and the action of pulling the lead causes the upper lip to open, displaying the teeth in a realistic manner and giving every appearance of a smile. This is an excellent movement to have fitted to a figure.

CRYING. This simply consists of a double syringe terminating at two small holes bored above each eye. The syringe is charged with water and made detachable for filling purposes. The head of the doll is held forward and by pressing the bulb of the syringe a flow of " tears " is produced. I do not recommend this movement, for quite apart from the liability to damage the figure, it is hardly desirable for use in drawing-room entertainments.

MOVABLE ARMS. The lower portion of the arm is fitted with a thin iron rod. This rod is set in prolongation of the arm and then bent at a right-angle, and so the end is concealed behind the body. A small wooden handle is fitted by which the figure's arm can be made to move in almost any direction. The disadvantage here is that the performer has to temporarily leave go of the mouth lever to work the arm.

A similar movement can be fitted to the legs.

There are several other movements which I do not consider it worth while to describe, such as, protruding tongue, flapping ear, elongated neck, etc. etc.

Of course, different manufacturers of ventriloquial figures are bound to vary the mechanism, but this list is given to serve as a general description.

I do not consider it necessary to have a figure fitted with many movements beyond a good mouth movement. After all, it is a ventriloquial entertainment and not a marionette show that you propose to carry out.

MANIPULATION OF VENTRILOQUIAL FIGURES

To a certain extent a ventriloquist should have the abilities of an actor. Talking to a " doll " and receiving impertinent answers and remarks in return is only effective if the respective parts are acted. A good ventriloquist will use his figure so naturally that after a few lines of dialogue the audience will almost forget that the doll is not human. Even the performer himself will be lead to overlook the fact that he is only talking to an automatic dummy.

Figure manipulation resolves itself under three headings, viz. mouth movement, head turning movement, and general movement. The last being more or less a combination of the first two.

Now let me emphasise the first important point in good figure working. The figure must be kept in movement from the minute the performer appears on the stage until the final curtain. When the doll is not " talking " a very slight movement of the body and an occasional turn of the head will be sufficient, but never allow the figure to look what it really is, a mechanical automaton.

27

Many performers open their entertainment with
the figure seated on a chair or table in the centre
of the stage. The ventriloquist will enter on the
rise of the curtain and pick up the figure. Now
until he has seated the figure on his knee and
obtained possession of the ring or lever for working
the mouth, the automaton will appear unnatural.
To eliminate this the performer should always come
forward with the figure under his arm. As he
makes his bow the figure will look around the
audience. Having laid the foundation of the
illusion he is about to create, the performer should
quickly settle in a chair and commence the
dialogue.

Now let us consider the mouth movement. It
is useless to try and compare an automatic mouth
with a human one. The mouth of a ventriloquial
figure is not constructed to move laterally. Therefore it is necessary to open the mouth as the first
syllable of a word is produced and close it again
on the last sound of that word. If the word is a
long one the mouth must be made to open and
close two or three times, and if a short word to only
open and close once. As an illustration, the word
" yes " would only require one mouth opening,
whereas " Gentleman " would require three quick
openings. The set rule therefore is that the mouth
be made to open and close on each sounding
syllable of a word. With very little practice the

beginner will find himself actuating the mouth in absolute rhythm with the words spoken.

At this point let me again say how important it is to practise in front of a mirror, for it enables the performer to see the effect of his figure and ventriloquism, as seen by an audience.

Now for the movement of the head, which is most essential to eliminate any appearance of " stiffness " in the figure and also to create a humorous effect. As a method of instruction I will again describe a mistake made by many performers. The mistake is keeping the head of the doll facing the audience during the whole of the dialogue. It is absolutely necessary in creation of the perfect illusion to make the figure look up at the performer as a question is asked and then look back at the audience as it replies. At other points in the dialogue the figure can be made to glance around the audience, take a quick look at the orchestra or appear to be interested in some part of the stage. There are many similar humorous and effective movements, but more about this in a later article.

Having briefly described the movements of the automaton, let me now turn to the ventriloquist. I repeat that he must act, and the part he must play is one of indifference to the presence of the doll seated on his knee. When the doll is talking the ventriloquist should be looking at the audience or glancing casually and indifferently around the place. He must give the impression of having nothing to do with the voice or movement of the figure. Everyone knows that it *is* the ventriloquist who is producing the voice, but the art of ventriloquial figure working is to produce the perfect illusion. If the ventriloquist asks a question and then gazes intently at the doll as it answers, half the illusion is destroyed, for the audience imagine the ventriloquist is afraid the mouth of the doll is not working properly or that he is too conscious of a poor concealment of his ventriloquial voice. Again, if the performer continually looks at the figure, when it is speaking, it tends to lesson the imagination of the audience to such an extent that they will pay more attention to the face of the ventriloquist than to the movements of the doll. The result is a considerable loss of effect.

The following simple dialogue with bracketed instructions will serve to show the combination of acting and manipulation as described in the foregoing article :—

VENT. (*turning to* DOLL *at commencement of sentence and facing the audience again at the conclusion*). " There are a lot of people here to-night, my boy."

DOLL (*glances at performer—looks round audience and back to performer*). " Yes, Guv'nor," (*looks to front again*) " They have come

to see me " (*looks quickly up at performer*).

VENT. (*turning to* DOLL). "Nonsense." (*Looks to
audience*) " They have come to see me."

DOLL (*turning to performer and back to audience*).
" They will all want their money back
then."

I have purposely refrained from describing the
now almost extinct method of working a whole
row of figures seated across the stage. The modern
ventriloquist normally carries out his entertainment
with one figure only. The whole of my articles and
dialogues for Figure Entertainments will therefore
be devoted to the figure popularly known as " The
Cheeky Boy."

TABLE OF PRACTICE

FIGURE MANIPULATION

1. PRACTISE the general movements of the figure, especially the head-turning movement.

2. Produce single words with long and short syllables, actuating the mouth to synchronise as follows :—

Practise in succession the words " Go " (mouth of figure opens once), " away " (opens twice), and " Together " (opens three times).

3. Practise the sample lines of dialogue found in " Manipulation of Ventriloquial Figures," following the bracketed instructions given therein.

4. Carry out an " argument " with the Cheeky Boy, paying careful attention to the quick change from ordinary voice to ventriloquial voice and to the necessary acting.

Generally, have due regard to all that is written on Figure Manipulation when practising these exercises.

SPECIAL FIGURE MOVEMENTS

QUITE apart from witty dialogue and the use of special mechanical contrivances fitted to figures, which I have already explained, considerable amusement can be derived from various special methods of manipulating a figure. In good hands, a figure can be made to cause a laugh without a word being spoken. To give an example : I have seen a good ventriloquist carry his figure on to the stage, then sit down and appear to quite ignore the figure. During this time the Cheeky Boy indulges in a deliberate glance around the audience, then looks up at the performer and again back at the audience. This, before a word of dialogue, never fails to cause amusement, which is often followed by a further laugh when the boy, becoming impatient looks up and says : " Didn't you see me come on, Guv'nor ? "

I will suggest a few effects at random. Many more will occur to my readers who take figure manipulation seriously.

A capital effect is produced if the doll carries on a whispered conversation with the performer. After appropriate dialogue, the boy requests the

ventriloquist to come nearer to him. The head of
the doll is then turned in the direction of the performer's right ear, at the same time allowing the
face to be clearly visible to the audience. Now,
by short, sharp pulls of the lever or ring, the mouth
is made to open and close very slightly, the performer
looking interested and occasionally replying " Yes "
and " No," etc. The slight movement of the mouth
gives the figure the appearance of whispering.

The following effect reflects credit on the performer's figure manipulation although very easy
to do. A letter is suddenly " discovered " on the
table and the ventriloquist requests the boy to
be quiet while he reads it. After a short pause the
boy also looks down at the letter. Now if the mouth
is operated as in the whispering effect, the boy
appears to be reading the letter to himself and
quietly repeating the contents. Then the ventriloquist suddenly looks up and reprimands the boy
for his rudeness. This can be repeated several
times and on each occasion that the ventriloquist
glances up, the boy turns his head sharply in the
opposite direction, as though to convince the performer that he has never been reading the letter at
all.

If the ventriloquist is smoking during his entertainment he can blow a cloud of smoke at the boy's
face. This causes the boy to shake his head rapidly
several times, followed by a cough or a sneeze.

At regular intervals during the entertainment the boy can be made to yawn. This is carried out by slowly opening the figure's mouth to the full extent, at the same time pulling the head well back followed by several rapid shakes.

Should a person enter the hall in the middle of a performance the boy can be made to follow the person's movement until he is seated.

DIALOGUE AND STYLES OF VENTRILOQUIAL ENTERTAINMENT

To a great extent a dialogue must be written to suit the character of the figure in use. A dialogue written for a Boy Scout would be of little use, as a complete dialogue, for a coster figure. I say, as a complete dialogue, because a certain portion of the jokes and sayings might be adapted for use with almost any figure.

Originality and refinement should be the keynote, and the ventriloquist should always be on the lookout for the introduction of impromptu jokes (see " Impromptu Dialogue "). Smart topical quips are always appreciated, but the exclusion of personal jokes is advisable. An amusing and popular form of dialogue is a recitation attempted by the ventriloquist with frequent and witty interruptions by the figure.

Although it is essential that a dialogue be thoroughly learnt and rehearsed, it is a great mistake to deliver it in, shall I say, a " parrot-like " style ? In other words—be natural, and dispel the impression that the dialogue has ever been written or rehearsed.

Some performers are content to make up their dialogue with a collection of individual jokes or gags. As soon as one joke is finished they switch on to the next and spoil the appearance of natural conversation. It is at least necessary to blend one joke into the other and so avoid a too common repetition of such sayings as, " Oh, by the way," " That reminds me," etc.

A distinct improvement on the set style of dialogue is to compile the material at one's disposal in the form of a complete sketch or scena. In this case characters are created for both the ventriloquist and the figure and a certain amount of plot must creep into the dialogue. For example, I have written a sketch for this book entitled " Teddy, the Lift Boy." The ventriloquist plays the part of an hotel visitor and the figure is dressed to represent the Lift Boy. On the concert platform it is usually impossible to have appropriate scenery, but this can be imagined or explained on the programme. The plot of the sketch is as follows : The hotel visitor discovers the Lift Boy asleep in a chair. He is roused from his slumbers and made to answer certain questions in reference to the hotel. The visitor then explains that he is looking for his wife, who has preceded him and booked a room. After further dialogue, the Lift Boy confides in the visitor to the extent of telling him his latest romance. The conversation leads up to a point where the visitor discovers that Teddy has actually been making love to his wife. The boy is surprised when informed of this fact, but all complications are cleared away by a song from Teddy, which, as usual, concludes the sketch.

In later articles I also explain how ventriloquial mimicry and distant voice work can be mixed up with an ordinary dialogue and used in conjunction with the figure.

IMPROMPTU DIALOGUE

A GOOD performer can make a lot out of impromptu dialogue, inspired by any movements amongst the audience. For instance, a spectator who is rude enough to leave the hall in the middle of a performance can bring forth the remark from the Cheeky Boy, "There goes the first victim," or ". He knows I am going to sing in a minute." Such additions to the dialogue cause endless amusement and prove that the ventriloquist is a good and resourceful showman. Therefore the performer should be on the look-out for any happening that gives an opening for spontaneous remarks from the figure.

Often the programme attendant will pass along the front of the seats. The boy should be made to look over and ask, "How many have you sold, George?" This remark would, no doubt, be ignored by the person addressed, which would cause the figure to say, "Don't keep answering me back."

The possibilities of impromptu remarks naturally vary according to where the ventriloquist is performing. In a drawing-room it is often possible to address a good-natured quip to one of the best-known members of the audience.

If a man in the front row of the stalls lights a cigarette, the boy is made to vainly try to blow out the match, with dialogue such as the following :—

BOY (*to* GENT, *in stalls*). " Got any cigarette cards, Sir ? "

VENT. " I suppose you are aware that some brands of cigarettes do not have cards ? "

BOY. " Oh yes—Woodbines."

VENT. " Why do you want cigarette cards ? "

BOY. " To feed the rabbits with."

Many amusing asides may be introduced when performing with an orchestra. The boy leans over the footlights and addresses the conductor as follows :—

BOY. " Good evening, Mr. Conductor."

VENT. " Please do not address the Conductor."

BOY. " Which variety is he, ' Bus ' or ' Lightning ' ? "

VENT. " He conducts the orchestra."

BOY. " Where to ? "

VENT. " He is responsible for the music we have just heard."

BOY. " Then he ought to be ashamed of himself. Besides, he is not a real conductor."

VENT. " Why not ? "

BOY. " He hasn't long hair. (*To* BASS PLAYER) Look at that man with the overgrown fiddle."

VENT. " That is the bass."

BOY (*to* 'CELLO PLAYER). " What is yours? The small bass? "

VENT. " Who do you think is the best paid person in the orchestra? "

BOY. " The trombone player."

VENT. " Why? "

BOY. " Because he has the most *brass*."

VENT. " Do you play."

BOY. " Oh yes."

VENT. " I play the piano and organ. What do you play? "

BOY. " Football."

At a smoking concert where liquid refreshments are being served the boy can address many remarks to the waiters, such as, " Waiter, there are two of us up here." The boy could then follow every movement of the waiter until he left the room, and then remark, " Guv'nor, that man has no heart."

An imaginary umbrella laying against a vacant chair is " discovered " by the boy. Turning to the ventriloquist he will say, " Look, Guv'nor, a gentleman has gone out and left his umbrella." This is followed by a humorous whispered conversation with the figure during which the ventriloquist frequently shakes his head and says aloud, " No," or " It wouldn't do," after which the boy deliberately remarks aloud, " Well, it might rain going home to-night, Guv'nor."

An amusing reference may be made to the performer who is to follow the ventriloquist on the stage, or the artiste who preceded him. Remarks may be introduced about the stage, and in a variety of other ways smart asides can be introduced.

The scraps of dialogue contained in this article are merely suggestions on the general principles of impromptu work. I now leave the subject to the wit and ability of the performer.

SINGING

SINGING may be introduced into almost any class of ventriloquial entertainment and especially when performing with a boy figure. The audience will focus their attention on the performer, and the ventriloquist who has completely mastered the art of eliminating lip or face movements, will create an impression in making a song by the boy a feature of his entertainment. Only a short song is necessary, which must be selected with due regard to the character of the figure. During the song the performer should look at the audience and not even appear to be listening to the song. The figure should be kept in motion the whole time, not only by a well-synchronised mouth movement, but also with a slight swing of the head and an occasional glance up at the performer.

The introduction of a song gives scope for plenty of amusing dialogue of which the following is merely a sample :—

VENT. " Can you sing ? "

BOY. " I've never been accused of it."

VENT. " Surely you have learnt to sing—' doh, ra, me——' "

43

BOY. " Not ' sol, far.' "

VENT. "Can you sing 'Deep in a Rose Bud red?' "

BOY. " No—but I can sing ' Deep in a Cabbage green.' "

VENT. " Well, do you know ' Bonny Mary of Argyll ? ' "

BOY. " Not to speak to."

VENT. " Can you sing ' In the Merry Month of May ? ' "

BOY. " Not in October."

VENT. " Well—what will you sing ? "

BOY. " Drink to me only with thine Eyes—I've only tuppence left."

It is rather more difficult to introduce a song with an imaginary character, such as in a screen dialogue. In this case the performer has no figure with which to perfect the illusion and must rely entirely on his own gestures. So the part played by the ventriloquist must be exactly the opposite to the method employed when making a figure sing. Instead of appearing to ignore the singer, the necessary gesture must be introduced to suggest careful attention to every word that is being rendered. In other words, what I have written about screen dialogues applies equally to screen songs.

The performer will find it a great strain to sing in a distant voice and I only advise an item under this heading after considerable practice. The song must be very short and the musical accompaniment soft and slow. Naturally, the procedure of presenting a distant song is the same as the presentation of a distant voice dialogue.

"A NOVEL CRITIC"

DIALOGUE FOR CHEEKY BOY

VENT. " Are you any good as a critic ? "

BOY. " I always get bowled first ball."

VENT. " I said ' critic,' not ' cricket.' Now
listen to me."

BOY. " That's what I keep on doing."

VENT. " I want all your attention."

BOY. " You can't have it—I haven't brought it
all with me."

VENT. " Lend me your ears for a moment."

BOY. " I can't—they're a fixture."

VENT. " You misunderstand me. I have a little
matter on hand——"

BOY. " Which hand ? "

VENT. " I want your co-operation——"

BOY. "—want me to go under an operation ? "

VENT. " No ! No ! I want you to get me out of
a difficulty."

BOY. " How much do you owe ? "

VENT. " It is not a matter of money."

BOY. " There is not to be a wedding then ? "

VENT. " What do you mean ? "

46

Boy. " Matter-o-money " (matrimony).

Vent. " The fact is, I am writing a novel and I require your assistance."

Boy. " What does the novel consist of ? "

Vent. " Why brains, my boy. Are you surprised to hear that ? "

Boy. " Not a bit. There are none in your head so they must be somewhere."

Vent. " Now first of all, what is a novel ? "

Boy. " A bob's worth of paper to wrap up fish and chips."

Vent. " A novel is a representation sustained by characters."

Boy. " A presentation obtained by characters ? "

Vent. " Now every novel must have a title."

Boy. " What is yours ? An Earl or Duke."

Vent. " Then you must have a plot."

Boy. " What's wrong with an allotment ? "

Vent. " The plot is the theme."

Boy. " So it ' themes.' " (Vent. *opens book.*)

Vent. " The scene is laid in Devonshire."

Boy. " Who laid it ? "

Vent. " The heroine is a pretty girl named Maud."

Boy. " Case of ' Come into the Garden, Maud.' "

Vent. " No ! No ! "

Boy. " The allotment then ? "

Vent. " There is no question of Maud going into the garden."

Boy. " Then take the garden in to Maud."

VENT. (*reading*). " In chapter one, Maud is kidnapped."

BOY. " You're kidding."

VENT. " She has been trapped by brigands."

BOY. " That's a trifle strong for chapter one."

VENT. "——She is trying to effect an escape——"

BOY. " Couldn't she disguise herself as a pot of Devonshire cream ? "

VENT. " Talk sense."

BOY. " Avez-vous de la monnaie ? "

VENT. " What are you doing ? "

BOY. " Talking French."

VENT. " As I was trying to tell you—In chapter one, Maud is alone in a locked building."

BOY. " She can't be alone."

VENT. " Why not ? "

BOY. " There is a man there."

VENT. " What man ? "

BOY. " Chap ; One."

VENT. " Now these are Maud's lines."

BOY. " Well, I don't want them."

VENT. (*reads*). " I am caught like a rat in a trap. How can I escape ? "

BOY. " Eat the cheese."

VENT. " But what is that I see ?—A loose brick— How came that here ? "

BOY. " Someone threw it at you."

VENT. " This is dramatic."

BOY. " It's worse than that."

VENT. " Listen to these words : ' A lump rose in her throat—What should she do ? ' "

BOY. " Swallow it."

VENT. " Suddenly she heard music——"

BOY. " A German band."

VENT. " No ! "

BOY. " ——waist band."

VENT. " She listened to the music. She was in wonderment."

BOY. " Thought you said she was in prison ? "

VENT. " She pulled at the iron bars that covered the small window. The music came nearer and nearer."

BOY. " Couldn't she slip out between the ' Bars ' ? "

VENT. " Then she heard footsteps outside. Who was it ? "

BOY. " The Bandsmen coming for a collection."

VENT. " She must not be seen. What should she do ? "

BOY. " Hide behind the brick."

VENT. " The stranger entered. Who was this man ? "

BOY. " Chap ; One."

VENT. " He saw her standing there."

BOY. " *Must* have had good eyesight."

VENT. " He gazed at her form."

BOY. " Was she sitting on it ? "

VENT. " No ! No ! There was no form to sit on."

D

BOY. "I see—just plain *board* and lodgings."

VENT. "Of course, the man fell in love with her."

BOY. "Of course."

VENT. "Now in Chapter Two they become engaged, in Chapter Three they are married——"

BOY. "I will tell you what I should like to know?"

VENT. "Yes."

BOY (*leaning over and in a loud whisper*). "What happens in *Chapter Four?*"

TABLE OF PRACTICE

THIRD STAGE

ADVANCED VENTRILOQUIAL FIGURE-WORKING

1. PRACTISE any figure movements as explained in " Special Figure Movements."

2. Practise a short dialogue, devoting careful and long study to all the points mentioned in the previous table.

3. Practise samples of impromptu dialogue.

4. Study a short ventriloquial song. Having become proficient in the production of ventriloquial speech, it is only a small step forward to create a singing voice. This, therefore, requires no further explanation.

5. Practise the complete dialogue " A Novel Critic." This dialogue is specially written for the beginner.

CARE OF VENTRILOQUIAL
FIGURES

I FEEL that a few words on this subject will not
be superfluous, especially when I relate the following
personal experience. On one occasion, in my early
days as a ventriloquist, I commenced to operate
my figure in the usual way. When I pulled the lever
to open the mouth I found that the mouth would
not close again. With my disengaged hand I forced
the mouth back and pulled it open again with the
same result. To my absolute dismay I then found
that the mouth refused to work at all, although the
spring and lever appeared to be perfect. I therefore
had to beat a most undignified retreat, to the
accompaniment of several doubtful remarks from
certain members of the audience. On a close
examination I discovered the defect. Previous to
this particular engagement I had stored my figure
in a damp room, with the result that the movable
portion of the mouth had become considerably
swollen. . . . Consequently, when it was pulled
down it came in contact with the sides of the face
and the enlarged condition resulted in it sticking
firmly.

There are two morals to this. Firstly, always keep the figure in a dry place, and secondly (although this away from the subject), be prepared in this, or any other emergency, with an alternative item, such as a curtain dialogue or a demonstration of distant voices.

Care must also be taken of the springs. The periodical application of a little oil will eliminate any creaking and at the same time preserve the springs.

Cords and levers actuating the various movements of the figure must have constant attention. The cords are liable to wear with continual use, and as soon as they become only slightly frayed it is safest to renew them.

In packing the figure for transport it is always advisable to disconnect the shaft to prevent it becoming strained. (This would cause the head to work loosely on the base of the shaft.) The head should be securely wrapped in innumerable pieces of paper, also the hands and legs.

VENTRILOQUIAL MIMICRY

As this book is written exclusively on the subject of ventriloquism I only propose to explain the art of mimicry, so far as it can be used in an entertainment with a ventriloquial figure. Mimicry, within the true meaning of the word, has nothing at all to do with ventriloquism, although perhaps it can be termed a "Sister Art." Therefore, the items I submit are so arranged that the ventriloquial figure is the "mimic," and hence the above title.

SAWING WOOD. Close the teeth tightly and press the tip of the tongue against the top of same. Take a deep breath and let the air out again in short "grunts," to the accompaniment of a low varying musical hum. Remember that the figure is supposed to be doing the imitation, so the lips of the performer are immobile. During the production of the sound, the figure's mouth is made to open and close very slightly with a corresponding turn of the head.

PLANING WOOD. The teeth and tongue are in the same position as in sawing wood, but the air is discharged at the sides of the mouth in a series of drawn-out hisses. The head of the figure is made to turn

from right to left, as though following the movement
of the plane.

BEE. Again the teeth and tongue are in the same
position, and as the air is expelled from the mouth
a continual musical buzz is produced, increasing in
volume as the bee appears to come nearer and
gradually becoming softer as it flies away. The
heads of both the doll and the performer must follow
the imaginary flight of the bee as it appears to travel
around the stage.

BANJO. The nearest sound to a banjo note is
" pang," but as this is impossible to clearly pronounce in a ventriloquial voice, the phonetic sound
of " tang " is substituted. This is delivered rapidly
in a musical note, with the teeth closed, clearness of
sound being obtained by striking the tongue on the
roof of the mouth. The mouth of the figure is made
to open and close slightly as each " tang " is produced, with the necessary movement of the head in
rhythm.

DOG. The bark of a dog is best produced from
the back of the throat, and the beginner will find
that it requires some little practice and control to
deliver it ventriloquially. The following instructions should be sufficient to convey the principles of
producing the required sound. With the teeth
lightly closed and the lips open, make an ordinary
musical note, at the same time expelling the air from
the mouth. Then reverse the process by continuing

the note, but drawing in the breath instead. This
will carry the sound to the back of the throat. Now
change the note into a series of sharp grunts, still
breathing in as before. It is then only a matter of
practice to develop the grunt into a bark. In
actually presenting the imitation, the doll's mouth
must be made to open and the head jerked back as
each successive bark is emitted.

OPENING A BOTTLE OF WINE. This is an effective
yet easy item, permitting some amusing preliminary
dialogue, which can be worked quite naturally with
the figure. The imitation consists of drawing an
imaginary cork and then pouring liquid (also
imaginary) from bottle to glass. The " pop " of the
cork is produced by pressing the tongue tightly
against the roof of the mouth and then drawing it
away very sharply. The sound of the liquid passing
through the narrow neck of the bottle is made by
a series of sharp movements of the tongue against
the roof of the mouth.

I submit the following dialogue to show how such
an item should be introduced :—

VENT. " I want you to give an imitation of open-
　　　ing a bottle of wine."
BOY. " *Only* an imitation ? "
VENT. " It is purely imaginary."
BOY. " In the menagerie ? All right—I'll draw
　　　the cork. (*Head of figure is pushed*

slightly forward, turned from side to side several times and jerked up again as sound is produced of cork leaving bottle.) Just like the real thing—quite thirst provoking."

VENT. " Now imagine the liquid is being poured into a glass." *(Imitation as described. Head of figure is made to nod slightly in support of the imaginary action.)*

BOY. " An imaginary ' Good Health,' Guv'nor."

It is almost impossible to describe in detail the action of the vocal organs in the accomplishment of mimetic sounds. My advice to beginners is to study sounds from real life. For instance, a few hours spent in a farmyard is the best and easiest way of acquiring the art of animal mimicry.

It is not necessary to confine this class of entertainment to the imitation of sounds. Considerable effect can be obtained from imitations of street hawkers, canvassers, children, speeches, etc. ; all rendered by the figure.

These examples, however, should be sufficient for the beginner to master the principles of ventriloquial mimicry and strike out for himself on any original lines that may occur to him.

DISTANT VOICE PRODUCTION

To the uninitiated there is an implicit belief that a ventriloquist can " throw his voice." It is absolutely impossible for any person living to actually throw his voice. This may surprise many readers of that evergreen but entertaining book, *Valentine Vox*. Could any person be possessed of the extraordinary powers of ventriloquism attributed to Valentine Vox, a large fortune and unlimited fame would certainly be his. No! dear readers, voice throwing is impossible, but a trained ventriloquist can make his voice APPEAR to come from a distant object under certain conditions. Therefore the term " distant voice " is more applicable than " voice throwing."

The essential condition of distant voice production is that there must be a clear space between the performer and the object from which the voice is supposed to come from. A performer with people standing all around him could not possibly make his voice appear to come from anywhere the other side of those people. It is quite impossible because the " line of sound " between the performer and the distant object is intercepted by the human ear and therefore the sound can only appear to come from the ventriloquist himself, however good may be the voice produced.

So a ventriloquist who has the benefit of a stage or platform can introduce a larger variety of distant sounds than a performer in a drawing-room. But although the drawing-room entertainer is handicapped by lack of space, it need not prevent him from carrying out some quite effective distant voice work, even though his task is much more difficult than the stage artist.

Now for a most important point. I have already emphasised under " Manipulation of Ventriloquial Figures " how important it is for the ventriloquist to act his part. In distant voice production this is even more important, in fact, it is essentially the keynote of the whole art. The performer must stimulate the imagination of his audience. As an illustration, let me describe the right and wrong way of acting a distant voice item.

The performer opens the item by standing a few yards away from, say, a cupboard, telling the audience that there is a man inside. Then in a normal voice the ventriloquist says, " Are you there ? " Faintly comes the reply, " Yes, and I want to get out." Let us imagine that when this sentence is produced the performer casually looks into the audience. Then the whole effect is spoiled. Why ? Because the performer did not in any way act his part or lead the imagination of the audience towards the cupboard.

Obviously, then, this is the wrong procedure. Now for the right method which I set with appropriate dialogue, together with instructions as to gesture. The vital importance of acting should then be clear.

VENT. " Ladies and Gentlemen—you will be surprised to hear that there is a man imprisoned in this cupboard (*indicates cupboard by a glance at same*). I will call him. (*Then in a louder voice*) Are you there? (*Knocks or shakes cupboard door.*) (*A pause—the performer holds his hand to his ear and appears to be carefully listening, at the same time gazing intently in the direction of the cupboard.*) (*Distant voice*) Yes, and I want to get out*" (ad lib.*).

That is the right way, and I am sure my readers will have no difficulty in grasping the difference between right and wrong. Notice that when the performer addresses the imaginary man, he raises his voice to do so. A man in a closed cupboard could not be expected to hear the call in a normal voice.

Likewise, if you are speaking to a man down in the cellar, look towards the floor as you receive the reply. If the man is supposed to be walking about the cellar allow the eyes to travel slowly over the floor in the imaginary direction. Again, if the call comes from the roof, glance up at the ceiling, and at the same time move about the stage in an endeavour to catch sight of the person through the " skylight." It is this careful study of every detail that creates the perfect illusion. I refer in this case to the illusion of sounds.

Apart from the acting required on the part of the ventriloquist, I particularly request my readers not to connect this class of entertainment with anything I have written about ventriloquism with figures. Some of the principles are entirely different, for whereas an automaton is in itself the biggest asset to leading the imagination of the audience, in distant voice work the whole creation of the illusion rests entirely with the ventriloquist.

Then again, you are told to look away from a ventriloquial figure when it is supposed to be speaking. It will be noticed that with the " man in the cupboard " you are told to look at the cupboard. Why? Because the man in the cupboard is imaginary, the " cheeky boy " is not.

I have purposely dealt first with the presentation of distant voice items. Now for the production of the voice.

So far, I have only dealt with the creation of the ventriloquial voice for use with a figure. Many people will now say that it is only necessary to produce the same voice in a subdued tone, and it will sound distant to the audience. To a limited extent only is this correct. Although ventriloquial speech (for figures) is produced without movement of the lips and in an assumed voice, yet it should be produced with no more effort than is required to talk in the ordinary way. (Due allowance having been made for practice.)

Now to make that voice appear distant it is necessary to carry the sound to the back of the throat and FORCE it out from there. Therefore a distant voice is a strained voice requiring a certain reserve of breath.

My readers will appreciate the difficulty of describing in detail how such a voice is produced, so in an attempt to make it quite clear to the beginner, I give the following instructions :—

In an ordinary ventriloquial voice produce a musical note. Hum this note for a few seconds and then slowly proceed up the scale until a fairly high (but not forced) note is obtained. Dwell on this note, at the same time take a deep breath, then emit the note and force the sound to the back of the throat. A deep breath will expand the chest, and by holding back the breath as much as possible, consistent with producing the note, the desired effect will be produced.

Having mastered this most important preliminary exercise, it is more or less easy to proceed step by step, giving careful attention to the table of distant voice practice contained herein. I feel that study of these tables is far better instruction than any number of paragraphs I may write on the subject.   I therefore close this article, dealing later in the book with the actual dialogue and methods of introducing distant voice effects into different kinds of ventriloquial entertainments.

TABLE OF PRACTICE

DISTANT VOICE PRODUCTION

1. Produce a musical note and convert it into a distant sound, as explained in "Distant Voice Production."

Regular practice of this most important exercise will harden the throat and perfect the production of preliminary distant voice work. It is the foundation of all future distant voice effects, and it is therefore impossible to devote too much time to this exercise.

2. Having mastered item No. 1, produce a short "distant" sentence, such as, "Let me out," continuing this practice until uniformity of voice is obtained.

3. Practise the same sentence, but vary the strength, commencing loudly and gradually decreasing in volume until the voice completely gives out.

4. Produce the same sentence in an ordinary voice, then in a ventriloquial voice, and then in a distant voice, changing quickly from one to the other each time the sentence is repeated.

This is the best method of practising and mastering the art of changing from one voice to the other.

5. Practise the change of voices in the middle of this sentence as follows : " I want to get (*change to distant*) out of this cellar."

Stimulate the imagination by opening and closing either a door or the lid of a box, as the change of voice is effected.

6. Carry out a general study of the article on " Ventriloquial Mimicry."

SCREEN VENTRILOQUISM

WITH DIALOGUES

THIS class of ventriloquism consists of carrying on a dialogue with an imaginary person or persons behind a screen placed in the middle of the stage. For ordinary purposes the voice required is the same as with an entertainment with figures, but the presentation is much more difficult. Here again, as in every kind of ventriloquism, acting plays a most important part. The dialogue requires a bold presentation to lead the audience, for the time being, to almost feel there is actually a man behind the screen.

My instructions on distant voice production apply equally to screen ventriloquism, for the gesture is exactly the same. Therefore I do not consider it necessary to write any further instructions, but to proceed with a short dialogue in which it will be noticed that distant voices can naturally be introduced also under this heading.

VENT. " Ladies and Gentlemen,—Behind this screen (*indicates same*) is seated a very interesting and well-known country

66

gentleman. Dear old Farmer Giles. I am afraid he is rather nervous of facing the public and will not move from his concealment. (*Steps back and looks behind the screen.*) Ah! He has become tired of waiting for me and has fallen asleep. I must wake him. (*Bangs screen, glances behind and smiles.*) Here I am, Giles. How are you ? "

GILES. " Beg pardon ? "

VENT. (*to audience*). " Farmer Giles is rather deaf. (*To* GILES) Is that not so ? "

GILES. " Yus."

VENT. " You cannot hear what I say ? "

GILES. " That depends."

VENT. "——on what ? "

GILES. " On what you say."

VENT. " Would you like to start work now ? "

GILES. " Beg pardon ? "

VENT. (*louder*). " Would you like to start work now ? "

GILES. " Beg pardon ? "

VENT. " Would — you — like — to — start — work—now ? "

GILES. " Beg pardon ? "

VENT. (*softly*). " Would you like a drink ? "

GILES (*quickly*). " Yus ! "

VENT. " You are very smart."

GILES. " And very thirsty. Say, Guv'nor—? "

VENT. " What do you want ? "

GILES. " That drink."

VENT. " Oh, leave that alone."

GILES. " Oi baint touched it yet."

VENT. " I want you to go down the cellar." (*Indicates stage behind screen.*)

GILES. " Beg pardon ? "

VENT. " I want you to go down the cellar."

GILES. " Beg pardon ? "

VENT. " There is a barrel of beer at the bottom of the cellar which I want you to produce."

GILES. " Orlrite."

VENT. " Let me assist you."

GILES. " I don't want no 'sistance."

VENT. (*goes behind screen and looks down*). " Now be careful—steady. Now you are on your way."

GILES (*very slightly fainter*). " I'll soon get down."

VENT. (*looking down and in a louder voice*). " You will know when you are at the bottom."

GILES. " Yus ! I'll see the barrel."

VENT. " Are you nearly there ? "

GILES (*fainter*). " Yus." (*This question and answer is repeated several times, the reply " Yus " becoming fainter and fainter.*)

VENT. " Ah ! He has arrived at the bottom and will be fully occupied for the next hour so I may as well close the cellar door. (*Bangs foot on stage to indicate closing.*)

Giles is now thoroughly happy. (*Stamps foot on ' cellar door ' to attract attention.*) Giles ? "

GILES. " Hullo ! " (*very distant*).

VENT. " Are you enjoying yourself ? "

GILES (*distant*). " Not arf—good 'ealth—good 'ealth." (VENTRILOQUIST *comes forward and makes his bow.*)

The word " What ? " can be substituted for " Beg pardon " if the performer finds it difficult to clearly pronounce the latter.

Now for a screen entertainment introducing two or more characters. It is obviously essential that every character must have an entirely different and distinguishing voice. Therefore the performer must be familiar with various dialects. A good effect is produced with an old man and a small boy, and as a climax to the dialogue the old man appears to force the boy down the cellar. In addition to the dialogue between the ventriloquist and the respective characters behind the screen, the man and boy are made to argue between themselves much to the " amusement " of the ventriloquist. The effect can be quite imagined if the performer has completely mastered the art of keeping lips and face immobile.

To heighten the effect it is as well to have a pair of rusty hinges concealed on a ledge behind the screen, so that when the performer assists in opening the cellar, the hinges are heard to creak.

The Old Man is very gruff and abrupt, and as a contrast the boy has a squeaky voice and is addicted to stuttering.

The presentation and dialogue should be on the following lines :—

VENT.	" Ladies and Gentlemen,—I have two very amusing people behind this screen (*looks behind*). Ah ! There is Mr. Brown. Good evening."
BROWN.	" Is it ? "
VENT.	" And there is Timothy. How are you this evening ? "
TIM.	" Q-q-quite w-w-well."
BROWN.	" Just like a duck."
VENT.	" And how is Mr. Brown ? "
BROWN.	" Orlrite."
TIM.	" M-m-Mr. B-B-Brown, what makes y-your n-nose so r-red ? "
BROWN.	" The cold wind, my boy."
VENT.	" You must look after yourself this weather."
TIM.	" T-try a d-drop of c-cold w-wind."
BROWN.	" Shut up ! "
TIM.	" Shan't ! "
BROWN.	" 'Ere, help me open this 'ere cellar."
VENT.	" What for ? "

BROWN. " I'm going to put this kid out of his misery."

TIM. " I-I d-don't w-want to g-go down the c-cellar."

BROWN. " An' I don't want you to stop up 'ere. (VENT. *goes behind screen and assists man to open cellar, with frequent protests from the boy.*) Now, me lad, down you go."

VENT. " Be careful."

TIM. " I-I d-d-don't want t-to g-go down the c-cellar. (TIM *continues this remark, which gradually becomes fainter. Then the ventriloquist appears to be closing the door. Very faint*) I-I w-want to c-come up."

BROWN. " You can't. I'm standing on the lid."

VENT. (*looking down and shouting*). " Are you at the bottom ? "

TIM. (*very distant*). " Y-yes. . . . G-good-bye. . . . G-good-bye."

To elaborate this class of entertainment the ventriloquist can be equipped with a specially made piece of scenery, containing a door and window. The ventriloquist can open the door and argue with persistent canvassers, or sit under the window and hear street callers outside. In some of these items the performer may only appear to be an interested listener. For instance, a neighbour's quarrel may be enacted outside, without a remark from the ventriloquist, other than when introducing the item. During the quarrel the performer sits by the window, smoking or reading, and allowing the audience to see his lips the whole time. Needless to say the effect is excellent and loud applause assured. Of course, it is necessary to open the item with a few words suitably arranged to lead the imagination of the audience towards the open window and the characters assumed to be standing outside.

The following dialogue will serve as a sample :—

INTRODUCTION

VENT. (*crossing to chair under window*). " How nice it is when the day's work is over to sit by the *open window* and enjoy a smoke (*or read*). . . . (*Suddenly appearing to notice people outside*) Hallo ! It looks as though my peace is going to be disturbed to-day, for here comes Sally Briggs and Phœbe Smith having a quarrel as usual. Those people always insist on settling their differences underneath *my* window (*looking further out of window and withdrawing head quickly*). Here they are. Now we *shall* hear a row."

(SALLY BRIGGS *has a deep voice and* PHŒBE SMITH *a shrill, squeaky voice.*)

(During the ensuing argument the performer sits back in his chair and listens attentively to all that is being said, occasionally smiling at a remark and sometimes slightly lifting his head as though unable to hear certain words. These and other similar actions support the illusion.)

SALLY. " You ain't no good, Phœbe Smiff, an' yer ole man's no good, an' yer kids are urchins."

PHŒBE. " An' the same to you, Mrs. Briggs, an' all yer relations."

SALLY. " Look at yer ole man. Just look at 'im."

PHŒBE. " I'd like to. He ain't been 'ome for a week."

SALLY. " Shouldn't think so neither."

PHŒBE. " Yer thinks yer a lidy, dontcher ? "

SALLY. " I knows as 'ow I am."

PHŒBE. " An' I knows as 'ow yer ain't, even if your bruvver is in a butcher's shop."

SALLY. " You're a—you're a—a—woman."

PHŒBE. " An' you ain't. (*At this point the* VENTRILOQUIST *takes an apple from his pocket and throws it out of the window.*) 'Ere, who are yer chucking at ? "

SALLY. " Garn, I ain't chucked nuffink."

PHŒBE. " I saw yer do it. Chucked a tater or somefink. Now yer won't 'ave anyfink left for dinner."

SALLY. " Oh, shut yer clock."

PHŒBE. " Yer couldn't shut yours if you tried."

SALLY. " Your dial is like Big Ben."

PHŒBE. " An' yours is like a road after a steam-roller has bin over it."

SALLY. " Yer ain't even eddicated like me."

PHŒBE. " Fer two pins I'd scratch yer."

SALLY. " I wouldn't waste two pins on you."

(*At this point the* VENTRILOQUIST *slams the window in exasperation.*)

PHŒBE (*distant voice*). " You're no lidy. You're a cat."

SALLY. " You ain't nuffink." (*Similar argument continued until the voices die away.*)

A further improvement could be effected if the performer opens and closes the window several times, during the argument, thus demonstrating the quick change from normal to distant voice and vice versa. Another method is for the performer to eventually join in the quarrel and order the two people to move away, as follows :—

VENT. (*looking through window*). " Now look here ! I have had enough of this."

PHŒBE.   " I was only 'aving a little friendly chat
              with Mrs. Briggs, Sir."
VENT.   " Quite so.   But please finish your
              er—friendly chat elsewhere."
SALLY.   " Orlrite, Sir.   Come on, *dear* Mrs.
              Smiff."   (*The* VENTRILOQUIST *closes
              the window—a pause—then very dis-
              tant voice*) You're a cat—that's what
              you are."
PHŒBE.   " An' so are you " (*ad lib.*).

It will be noticed that Screen Dialogues give much
scope for a variety of effects, but I never advise a
longer " conversation " than five minutes with each
character introduced.

DISTANT VOICE WITH
A VENTRILOQUIAL FIGURE

IN a variety of ways the distant voice may be effectively introduced into an ordinary ventriloquial entertainment with a figure. The cheeky boy can be made to produce certain distant voices, which is a far better method than a complete distant voice entertainment without any figures.

During the entertainment the ventriloquist takes exception to a cheeky remark from the boy and places his hand over the mouth of the figure, as though to restrain him. Then comes the muffled (distant) cry: "Take your hand away—Take your hand away," etc. As the hand is withdrawn the voice becomes normal. This item can be carried out in the middle of a sentence providing the ventriloquist has mastered the art of quickly changing from normal to distant voice.

The following dialogue should make this movement clear :

VENT. " I have had enough of your impudence."
BOY. " I haven't."
VENT. " I did not come here to talk to a fool."

Boy. " I did ! " (Ventriloquist *claps hand over figure's mouth. The head is made to shake and twist as though the boy is trying to get clear of the performer's hand.*)
(*Distant voice*) " Take your hand away. Take your hand away."

Vent. (*withdrawing hand*). " Now be quiet."

Boy (*gasping*). " That was a nasty handful, Guv'nor, you (*hand again on mouth*)— *distant voice*) nearly choked me."

A similar change from normal to distant voice can be carried out during a song. This is very effective if properly executed.

One of the most popular items is " The Boy in the Box." Under " great provocation " the performer places the boy in a box or a suit-case. After some argument the box is closed, then in a distant voice the boy cries—" Let me out. Let me out." The effect created always calls forth loud applause and in addition to being very amusing, it suggests clever distant voice production. The effect is easy to carry out, requiring a certain amount of gesture. To greatly elaborate the item, the boy can be made to sing in the box, the sound becoming fainter as the lid is closed and louder as the lid is raised again. The voice is the same as produced when placing the hand over boy's mouth.

The following dialogue, with instructions in

brackets, will enable the beginner to master this excellent item :—

VENT. " If you say another word I shall place you in that box." (*Indicates box on stage.*)

BOY. " Who is going to help you ? " (*Glancing at box several times.*)

VENT. " I will show you." (*Crosses to box and lays* BOY *inside.*)

BOY. " No flowers, by request, Guv'nor. (*The* BOY *is now out of sight of the audience, so no mouth movement is necessary.*) Here, tuck my ' tootsies ' in." (*Feet are tucked into box.*)

VENT. (*glancing at* BOY). " Now I am going to close the box."

BOY. " That will put the lid on it. (VENTRILO-QUIST *closes the box and leans towards it as though straining ears to catch any sound from within. Distant voice*) Let me out. . . . Let me out. I want to get out."

VENT. (*speaking louder, for sound to penetrate box*). " You will remain where you are until you decide to behave yourself." (*After a pause, the lid is slightly raised.*)

BOY (*now normal voice*). " Why can't you let me out. I don't—(*lid closed again, distant voice*)—like it in here. Oh, let me out " (*ad lib.*).

The above is a good method of closing a performance. The boy is made to say " Good night " repeatedly, as the lid is gradually closed for the last time. The sound dies away as the performer comes to the front of the stage to make his bow.

With further practice the boy can be made to imitate street hawkers as they pass down an imaginary street. The heads of both the performer and the figure must gradually turn in the direction of the sound, as the voice becomes fainter and fainter, until it dies away altogether. The mouth of the boy is worked in the ordinary way and appropriate dialogue must accompany this rather difficult effect.

VENT. " You say you are good at imitating the cries of street hawkers ? Let me hear you give an imitation of a fish hawker, passing down the street." (*Indicate direction with left hand.*)

BOY. " That's easy, Guv'nor. (*Imitation of hawker's coarse voice.*) ' Fresh fish—all alive—all alive (*both follow direction. Fainter*). All alive—oh. Fresh fish (*fainter still*). 'Ere yer are—all alive— (*very distant*). Fresh fish——. (*Even fainter.*) Fresh—fish. (*Normal voice.*) He has sold out."

Then can follow imitations of the newsboy, fruit salesman, chimney sweep, and other familiar calls, too numerous to mention.

On the other hand, the performer himself can endeavour to present some distant voice items, with frequent interruptions from the boy. Let us imagine that the ventriloquist is supposed to be speaking to a man under the stage or down in a cellar.

VENT. " You may be surprised to hear that there is a man down in the cellar " (*indicates*).

BOY (*glancing down to floor and back to* VENTRILO-QUIST). " I expect he is ' pinching ' the pennies out of the gas meter."

VENT. " I will call him (*leans over and shouts loudly*). Hallo ! Hallo ! "

BOY (*sings well-known song*). " Who's your Lady Friend."

VENT. " Hush ! "

BOY. " Here comes the Bogey Man."

VENT. (*shouting*). " Hallo ! Hallo ! "

BOY. " I expect you are on the wrong line, Guv'nor."

VENT. " Are you there ? "

MAN (*distant*). " Yes, I'm here. May I come up ? "

VENT. " I beg your pardon."

MAN. " I want to come up."

BOY. " Show him the lift."

MAN. " I want to come up.   I want to come
          up."
BOY.   " I shall believe him in a minute."

Similarly, a conversation can be carried out with
a man on the roof or in a cupboard and in many other
ways the distant voice can be used to elaborate an
entertainment with a figure.

DRAWING-ROOM ENTERTAINING

I HAVE already said that it is much more difficult to present a ventriloquial show in a drawing-room than on stage or platform. Therefore a few remarks on Drawing-Room Entertaining will not be out of place.

However clever a performer may be, and however perfect in his Figure, the farther away he can get from his audience the better is the effect of his entertainment. If possible, a corner of the room should be selected and a screen borrowed, behind which the entertainment can be prepared. If, as is often the case, the audience show a desire to sit almost surrounding the performer, it is necessary to make a polite request that all chairs will be moved back as far as possible.

During the performance the figure should be kept as close as possible to the performer's head and careful study of environment is advisable before the introduction of distant voice effects. Under ordinary conditions I find that such items as " The Boy in the Box " and the business of placing the hand over Figure's mouth, can be carried out even in a small room. But such effects as the " man on the roof " are often impossible, and therefore best left for a stage show.

The Drawing-Room Entertainer is in a position to quickly study his audience and introduce dialogue accordingly, with due regard to any local impromptu jokes. Often there are children in the audience. Make the figure appear to notice them and call several of them by their Christian names. This never fails to please the juveniles and the popularity of the ventriloquist is assured.

COMBINING EFFECTS

HAVING now concluded articles on all the various subjects of the ventriloquial art, I am going to suggest a combination of these subjects, leaving further arrangements to the invention of the performer. A combination of effects would include ventriloquism with a figure, distant voices, ventriloquial mimicry, screen ventriloquism and singing, all in the one entertainment of, say, twenty minutes' duration.

The plot, if one can call it such, would be as follows : After some witty dialogue with the Boy, during which ventriloquial mimicry is incidentally introduced, the figure is placed behind a curtain in the centre of the stage. As soon as he is out of sight, the boy commences to annoy the performer, by interrupting a conversation on the telephone or during the time that the performer is trying to write or read a letter. (This introduces Screen Ventriloquism.) In exasperation the boy is removed from behind the screen and placed in the box (thus, distant voice). Then on condition that the precocious lad will sing, he is reinstated on the performer's knee and the show concluded with a short song.

TABLE OF PRACTICE

FIFTH STAGE

GENERAL COMBINATION

1. Practise the dialogue with a "man" in the cupboard, as explained in Distant Voice production.

2. Carry out a screen dialogue, devoting most attention to gesture and methods of presentation.

3. Practise ventriloquial mimicry.

4. Thoroughly practise distant voices with a figure, especially the "boy in box."

5. Rehearse and produce a dialogue, in which all effects are combined.

6. REMEMBER. Practice makes perfect.

Beyond this, the performer should devote his attention to the production of a ventriloquial sketch of about twenty minutes' duration, on any original lines.

"TEDDY, THE LIFT BOY"

A VENTRILOQUIAL SKETCH FOR BOY FIGURE

SCENE.—*Entrance to an hotel lift.*

At curtain the LIFT BOY *is in chair covered with a paper.*

VENT. (*entering with two bags*). "Ah—this must be the lift boy. It seems a pity to disturb him, but I must find my room" (*shakes figure*).

BOY (*from under paper*). "Don't wake me. I'm fast asleep."

VENT. "Come here, you lazy lad (*pulls paper away*). Is this the way you spend your time?"

BOY (*now seated on performer's knee*). "Not always, Sir. Sometimes I sleep on the sofa."

VENT. "And I notice you cover up your face with a copy of *Answers*."

BOY "Well, it 'answers' my purpose."

VENT. "Now where am I going to place my bags?"

BOY. "Continue wearing them, Sir."

VENT. "But I want my room."

Boy. " I haven't got it, Sir."

Vent. " Well, what is my number ? "

Boy. " Your ' number's ' up."

Vent. " What do you mean ? "

Boy. " Up the lift, Sir."

Vent. " But where is the lift ? "

Boy. " On the top floor, Sir."

Vent. " Then how can I get it ? "

Boy. " Go up to the top storey and push it down."

Vent. " You are very rude. Don't you know manners ? "

Boy. " Not to speak to."

Vent. " As a matter of fact, my wife has taken a room here."

Boy. " That's all right, Sir. You've time to slip away."

Vent. " Now please ring for the lift. What is the lift for ? "

Boy. " To take people up, Sir."

Vent. " And pray tell me, what are you for ? "

Boy. " To take people ' down,' Sir."

Vent. " You are very rude. How were you brought up ? "

Boy. " In the lift."

Vent. " You are very witty. Now what sort of a job is yours ? "

Boy. " Well, Sir, it has its ' ups and downs,' but on the whole it is fairly ' elevating.' "

VENT. " And do you get good money ? "

BOY. " Yes, Sir. The money is good, but there's very little of it. I rely on *tips*."

VENT. " Do you ? "

BOY. " Yes, Sir ; I absolutely rely on tips."

VENT. " Really ! "

BOY (*emphatically*). " A tip comes in very handy."

VENT. " I understand."

BOY. " Yes, Sir. I work much better with a tip."

VENT. " I suppose a half-crown would be quite useful ? "

BOY. " Yes, Sir (VENT. *produces a half-crown from left-hand waistcoat pocket, which he spins*). Tails, Sir."

(*The* VENTRILOQUIST *continues to spin the coin several times, every movement being eagerly followed by the figure — a pause.*)

BOY. "——er—very useful, Sir. (*The* VENTRILOQUIST *deliberately replaces coin in pocket.*) Have you made a mistake, Sir ? "

VENT. " No."

BOY. " Did you mean to do that, Sir ? "

VENT. " What ? "

BOY. " Show me your week's salary."

VENT. " Do you believe that money talks ? "

Boy. " Yes, Sir. I distinctly heard that half-
crown say ' Good-bye.' (VENTRILOQUIST
*now fumbles with right-hand waistcoat
pocket.*) You put it in the other pocket,
Sir."

VENT. " I am quite aware of that."

Boy. " So am *I*."

VENT. " Let's change the subject."

Boy. " Let's change the half-crown."

VENT. " If I gave you the coin you would not
know what to do with it."

Boy. " Would you like to experiment, Sir ? "

VENT. " Now tell me how you would spend the
money."

Boy. " I'd buy my girl some chocolates——"

VENT. " Yes ? "

Boy. "——and then eat them all myself."

VENT. " So you have a girl ? "

Boy. " I believe so, Sir."

VENT. " What **do** you mean ? "

Boy. " Well, Sir, there is a lady stopping at the
hotel that rather fancies me."

VENT. " Indeed ! "

Boy. " No, in the hotel. She gives me a button-
hole every day."

VENT. " And what have you done with to-day's
button-hole ? "

Boy. " Given it to my ' first reserve.' "

VENT. " So you have another girl ? "

BOY. " Must be prepared for emergencies, Sir."

VENT. " What room does this lady occupy ? "

BOY. " Here, do you want a button-hole as well ? "

VENT. " I am merely interested."

BOY. " Well, Sir, she is in Room Six. (VENT. *again places hand in waistcoat pocket.*) Don't do that, Sir."

VENT. " Why not ? "

BOY. " It reminds me of what might have been."

VENT. (*suddenly producing card*). " What is this ? "

BOY. " A pawn ticket."

VENT. (*examining card*). " Fancy me forgetting this. Why this is an hotel card with the number of my room on it (*again examines card*). Here, Boy. What number did you say the lady occupied ? "

BOY. " Number Six, Sir."

VENT. (*pushing card under figure's eyes*). " Well, look at the number of my wife's room on this card. What does it say ? "

BOY (*after much hesitation and head turning*). " S-s-six, Sir."

VENT. " So you have been paying attention to *my* wife. Explain yourself."

BOY (*aside*). " Now I am in a mess. (*To* VEN-

TRILOQUIST). You are looking at the card the wrong way up, Sir."

VENT. "I will humour you. Now I have reversed the card."

BOY. "Now you have the right number, sir—Number *Nine*."

VENT. "Yes—but if Number Nine is correct, how is it that the rest of the printing is *upside-down* ?"

BOY (*aside*). "Oh, Lor'. (*To* VENTRILOQUIST). Mistake of the printers', Sir."

VENT. "How do you feel now that you know I am the lady's husband ?"

BOY. "Very sorry."

VENT. "You really mean that ?"

BOY. "Yes, *very sorry*—for her."

VENT. "I feel almost inclined to laugh at the whole situation."

BOY (*aside*). "Good. (*To* VENTRILOQUIST.) Do laugh, Sir ?

VENT. "Ha ! Ah ! Ha !"

BOY. "I said 'laugh,' not try to swallow your face."

VENT. "It is such a joke that I almost wish I had given you that half-crown."

BOY. "So do I, Sir."

VENT. "After all, what is two and six ?"

BOY. "Eight."

VENT. " Now I will give you the coin if you will
sing me a song."

BOY. " Right-ho, Sir. That ought to bring
down the lift—and the curtain."

(Song to finish.)

IN CONCLUSION

AT last I find myself at the end of my subject. I have written as briefly as possible, avoiding superfluous explanations. If *every* detail had been written I should have filled twice this space. Therefore I trust that I have drawn the line at a point which will render the subject instructive, but nor boring.

I conclude with the hope that I have been successful in recruiting many new and promising students of the ventriloquial art.

HAROLD KING

72A HIGH STREET,
HASTINGS.

93

JUGGLING

BY

JOHN E. T. CLARK

JUGGLING

HOW TO GIVE A PERFORMANCE

Who has not come away from a concert, school entertainment or such-like performance with a strong desire to be able to do something out of the ordinary, something novel for an amateur to do and something really entertaining? This flame of ambition usually flickers out with the question asked of oneself, " What can I do ? " Now it may be that you are unable to sing or recite, although there is nothing really novel in possessing these acquirements after all ; therefore let me suggest that if you are possessed of average patience combined with the necessary ambition you practise up a Juggling performance. I am not, of course, going to propose that you attempt any such elaborate or costly tricks as are practised by some of the famous professional jugglers, but it is my present task to describe how you are to set about giving a really creditable little juggling performance aptly suitable for such entertainments as are mentioned above.

Many of my readers, I take it, have at some time or other learned to juggle with two or perhaps three articles, such as oranges, cricket balls or what not. Now with a little serious practice you will soon find yourself expert at juggling with three articles. You can then proceed to try four articles.

Learning to juggle is like learning to walk on stilts or to skim along on roller skates—if not already acquired it is a labour of love : the necessary practice is really enjoyable and most surely will be considered to be " all in the game." Personally I have known a beginner learn to juggle with six small wooden balls in two evenings, he practised in his bedroom and did about two hours each evening with short rests in between, and, it may be added, actually thought he was a long time learning, so that all things considered I am not expecting too much when I ask the keen aspirant to practise diligently simple juggling.

Although it is advisable for the novice to acquire skill in balancing or juggling various and diverse articles I strongly recommend him to commence with balls, preferably of wood, and about $2\frac{1}{4}$ inches in diameter and to practise a series of simple exercises, beginning with two only. The following will be found useful as an initial training for hand and eye, and the student will doubtless discover or invent others for himself :—

Exercise No. 1. Take a ball in each hand and

practise throwing both into the air simultaneously and catching them with the same hands.

Exercise No. 2. Alternatively throw a ball from the left hand into the air catching it with the same hand and repeat with the right hand.

Exercise No. 3. Throw a ball from hand to hand varying the distance, say, from 12 inches to 36 inches.

Exercise No. 4. Throw and catch the two balls alternately with one hand.

These exercises should be persisted in until the student is able to do them all steadily and with uniform precision and neatness, varying the height of the throw from time to time. I can honestly assure him that he will not find them tedious or boresome but, on the contrary, quite as good fun as tennis or cricket practice and, moreover, a most invaluable ground work for the more difficult seeming feats that follow.

I say advisedly *seeming*, because the novice will find that the practice of the foregoing and following exercise will lead so gradually and imperceptibly to the acquirement of the requisite dexterity and automatic precision of judgment that he will become an expert juggler without noticing the steps that have lead him to success.

It cannot, however, be too strongly emphasised that practice—at least an hour a day—should be persisted in steadily. Spasmodic practice—say, an hour to-day and another next week—is no use at all. It must be regular even if the time given to it each day is shorter than here prescribed.

Having mastered the above exercises the next step is to learn to juggle two, three, four or even five balls. Juggling with two balls is fairly simple and the procedure is as follows :—

Hold a ball in each hand, throw up the right-hand ball then throw the left-hand ball into the now unoccupied right-hand which now throws it up at the moment that the first ball is caught by the left hand. The whole operation is repeated *ad lib.* When you have learned to do this satisfactorily the juggling of three balls should next be attempted. In this case two balls are taken in the left hand and one in the right. The one in the right hand is first thrown up and immediately one of the left-hand balls is thrown into the right, and from thence in its turn into the air, the first ball thrown being caught in the left hand and immediately transferred to the right and so on.

Each ball should be thrown up to a fair height in order to obtain more time to pass the others in succession from the left hand to the right. The accompanying sketch (Fig. 1) will help you to understand the movements required.

It is essential that each ball should be thrown up to the same height and with the same strength, otherwise you will find that they return to the hand at irregular intervals and that you become flustered and drop them. This, however, together with accurate timing is a sheer matter of practice and the requisite knack is soon acquired.

The next step, juggling with four balls, should now present few difficulties. Commence with two balls in each hand—throw up first the two in the right hand one at a time, then throw the two in the left

FIG. I.

hand into the right also one at a time, these as they reach the hand each being thrown up in its turn, the principle is just the same in reality as in the manipulation of the three balls. The sketch (Fig. 2) may make matters clearer.

With regard to the choice of balls for use in your public entertainment the best are those of brass, sold for the purpose by Hamley's, Gamage's, or other well-known dealers in magical and juggling apparatus ; but there are many varieties in use. Many well-known professional jugglers use tennis balls.

In any case it is a sound principle not to use balls more than $2\frac{1}{4}$ inches in diameter or heavier than 4 ounces.

When you have attained to a sufficient degree of skill to be able to juggle four or five balls in the manner described above you should practise re-

FIG. 2.

versing the procedure, that is, throwing up the first ball with the left hand passing the others successively from right to left. It is highly important to develop skill in the use of the left hand equally with the right. There are of course many other objects which may be juggled with ; for instance, plates, straw hats, tambourines and other disc-shaped articles, to say nothing of Indian clubs, knives (specially prepared for juggling), top hats, etc.

The method of juggling round flat articles such as plates is much the same as applied to balls or other spherical objects, excepting for the added difficulty of keeping such things in a perpendicular position, as they must of course be thrown up edgeways (Fig. 3), and they are not quite so easy to transfer quickly from hand to hand. This again

FIG. 3.

can be surmounted by practice, and it is well worth the slight extra pains involved to acquire dexterity in the manipulation of such articles.

It is I suppose hardly necessary for me to mention that for juggling purposes the amateur and even the finished performer should use plates made from papier mâché—obtainable at any juggling out-fitter's—or even enamelled iron plates. The reason for this is of course obvious ; but apart from the risk of frequent breakages, the less fragile articles will be found much easier to manipulate than the china one.

There are many juggling feats which involve the use of three or more entirely dissimilar articles, differing largely not only in size and shape, but also in weight, as for instance Cinquevalli's feat of juggling with a cigar, an umbrella, a tall hat, a pair of gloves and a monocle, and the same artist's manipulation of two such widely differing objects as a steel cannon-ball and a screwed up cigarette paper.

In dealing with articles of different weights, shapes and sizes it is necessary to remember that each article must be thrown up in such a way and to such a height that it comes to hand at its correct time and in the correct position for handling. If, for instance, you are juggling with a silk hat, a suit-case and a cigarette, the suit-case must obviously be thrown to a greater height than the hat, and the hat higher than the cigarette, as the heavier article of course falls more rapidly than the lighter one.

Experiment and practice with such diverse articles as above mentioned will soon give you the necessary experience to judge accurately the rate of descent and the best angle for catching. I will assume that you have by assiduous practice on the foregoing suggested lines attained a creditable amount of experience and manipulative skill. Such being the case, the entertainment I am about to describe should be well within your powers of presentation.

As regards costume, this is of course largely a matter of taste; however, you should try and blend a little comedy with the performance, so I would suggest a clown's costume; or an old evening dress several sizes too large would do very well and should be easily obtainable. You would wear it with a large collar and a very large red bow. A clown's costume could be obtained at Gamage's or Messrs. Fox of Wellington Street, Strand, W.C., or hired or purchased from any similar firm of theatrical outfitters,

FIG. 4.

although such a costume could be easily manufactured at home (Fig. 4). In making up the face it is advisable to use white grease paint put on very thickly as the ground colour and afterwards to cover the nose and lips with carmine or ruddy rouge, or you may make a dot of black on each eyelid and eyebrow. The grease paint stick should first be

rubbed on and the colour afterwards worked all
over the face with the fingers. Always " blot out "
your own eyebrows completely for a clown's make-
up. There are, of course, various ways of making
up a clown's face. Examples are illustrated in Figure
5. You can if you wish omit the white ground, although I assure you that good grease paint is quite
harmless. You should prepare the face first by smear-
ing it all over with cocoanut oil removing the surplus

FIG. 5.

with an old towel. You will have to powder the face
after you have finished making up to take away the
shine. The face may be easily cleaned after the
performance with cocoanut oil and a towel. I will
now proceed straight away to describe the performance : you will require a table at the back of the
platform. This can be placed a little to one side
as to be out of the way. You will enter wearing a
silk hat, and as soon as the laughter which will greet
your appearance has subsided somewhat you take

from the table a walking-stick and proceed to balance
the hat crown downwards on the stick, which you
hold at right angles to the body (see Figure 6). This
is a fake, as of course you would not be able to do this
with an ordinary silk hat. Try it and see. You have
previously placed a circular piece of thick wood or
metal in the crown of the hat. This trick will be
very effective from the front. You now pretend to
get rather excited : you place the stick on the table

FIG. 6.

and quickly take from your pocket a large chunk of
bread, a carrot, and a bloater—the bloater can of
course be imitation, and may be purchased at any
theatrical outfitters for about a shilling—you juggle
with these three articles, working quickly as if you
were enjoying yourself immensely, and take an
occasional bite at the bread. You will have to stop
juggling for the moment to do this. After a while
you take from your pocket what appears to be a
small ball ; it is really an orange covered neatly
with white and coloured paper and previously

softened by banging it on the wall or table until it has almost burst. Now juggle with all four articles, and after a time catch the orange as it descends on your forehead. The splash that it will make will cause a yell of laughter from the audience, who will not be sure if it is a ball or not. You add to the fun by pretending that you are hurt, making grimaces and rubbing your head, etc. Needless to say you will not hurt yourself in the least, although if you are nervous you may use instead of the orange a soft rubber ball and get someone in the side to clap their hands as the ball strikes your forehead. You next place the bloater, carrot, and bread on the table—you are still wearing the hat—and picking up the ball or orange throw it up in the air in such a way that it falls behind your back (you are standing in the centre of the stage), then taking off your hat you hold it by the brim in front of you, crown downwards, and look up as if expecting the ball to drop into the hat. This will cause another laugh. You now pick up a long-handled carpet broom from the table and, standing in the centre of the stage, try to balance the broom, handle downwards, on your chin. Immediately you put the broom on your chin someone in the side fires a blank cartridge—a starter's pistol will do or a firework—and you then pretend to jump and replace the broom by the table. The next trick is the great Japanese umbrella and ball balance—this is where

you give the show away. Placing the hat upon the
table you pick up a large Japanese umbrella and a
coloured ball. The ball is about 2½ inches diameter
and is prepared thus : a small black wire ring is
attached to one end of a piece of black thread ;
the length of the thread should be less than half

PIN POINT ON
UMBRELLA HEAD

← END OF THREAD WITH
RING ATTACHED

HOLLOW BALL

FIG. 7.

the diameter of the umbrella when open. The other
end of the thread is fastened inside the ball which is
hollow and has a small hole to admit all the thread
leaving only the ring outside. The stick of the
umbrella has at the end of it a pin point protruding
about a ¼ of an inch (see Figure 7). You stand in the
centre of the stage, open the umbrella, stand the ball
upon the end of the stick and balance both on one

finger : although this looks difficult from the front
it is quite simple, as of course the ball is impaled
upon the pin.   You now lift the ball off and slip
the ring neatly over the stock, still holding the ball—
the thread will come out.   You then rapidly revolve
the umbrella, and the ball being now released
revolves round the edge of the umbrella.   You must

FIG. 8.

keep up the twisting and also dodge about a little
to give the idea that it is difficult to keep the ball
on the umbrella.   Keep this up a little while, then
suddenly close the umbrella and walk off the stage,
carrying the umbrella over your shoulder.   Of
course there will be a yell here from the audience,
as the ball will dangle in mid-air from the thread.
You turn your head just before reaching the side of
the stage and catching sight of the ball make a

dash and disappear. Re-entering you again pick up the carpet broom and try to balance it on your chin, someone at the side fires a blank at the critical moment as before and you pretend to jump and replace the broom by the table.

The trick that follows is somewhat novel, and to perform it you will require a board about 4 feet by 3 feet 6 inches. This board should stand near the centre of the stage, and can be leaned against the back of a chair (see Fig. 8). Any rough board will do and should be painted white. Now taking two balls from the table you proceed to bounce them against the floor and board one after the other as quickly as you can : the sound thus produced can be made to resemble the roll of a drum, the noise of a train, etc., according to the speed with which you manipulate the balls. If you can manage three or four balls you will get a wonderful effect as of a motor-car. After bowing your acknowledgment to the applause that is sure to follow this trick you replace the tennis

FIG. 9.

balls on the table and walk off the stage : you re-
enter carrying very carefully a bamboo pole about
8 feet long or longer prepared beforehand as
follows : Plug one end with a round piece of
wood, to fit tightly, now screw on to this a flat
thin board about 8 by 10 inches thus forming
a sort of pedestal (see Fig. 9). On this you
place a cup, tea-pot, and milk jug ; these should be
of enamel or tin or some such unbreakable material,
although it is best if they are coloured to look like
china. They are really attached to the pedestal
by means of lengths of thin twine : there should
be about a foot of loose twine. Tie these lengths
of twine on to the articles and make a loop in the
other end of each of these strings, pass a screw
through these loops and screw to the pedestal.
You carry the pedestal upright as you walk on to
the stage and very carefully lift it high enough to
enable you to place the other end on your chin.
You now try to balance this—if you really can
balance it so much the better—dodge about a great
deal to make believe it is a difficult trick, after a
little of this make your way towards the footlights
and pretend to stumble, contriving in doing so that
the pedestal falls outwards over the audience. Grip
the end of the bamboo tightly and " save " it just
as the tea-things are within a few inches of the
heads of the people sitting in the body of the
hall. Of course the tea-things will only dangle from

the end of the strings so no one will be hurt. You
will add to the excitement by giving a sudden yell
just at the critical moment when the pedestal is
falling. Carry the apparatus off and proceed with
the next trick.

Take up three large balls—about 4 to 6 inches in
diameter—two are of wood the third is of rubber:
all are painted the same colour; I would suggest
gold paint, but, of course, any colour will do. In
bringing them from the table you purposely drop
one of the wooden balls on the stage, this will give

FIG. 10.

the audience the impression that they are all solid
After juggling with these three for some moments,
you suddenly throw the rubber ball into the audience
—by the way be careful not to throw a wooden one—
at the same time catching one of the heavy balls
and dropping the other on the stage. There is sure
to be a yell here as the audience will think someone
is getting " brained." You now again pick up the
carpet broom and try to balance it on your chin,
someone fires a shot as before ; you shake your
fist towards the side and replace the broom by the
table.

The final trick, which is, of course, *the* trick of the

H

evening, is to roll a billiard ball on the edge of a cue.
The cue has to be prepared thus : Attached to the
tip by a tiny pin wire staple is a long loop of thin
black thread, the loop should be nearly as long as the
cue (see Fig. 10), just long enough in fact to slip over
the thumb of the right hand, the cue being held
almost at arm's length. Before commencing the
ball may be passed round for inspection ; if a real
billiard ball be used it must be the red one, although
any heavy ball will do, but it must be dark in colour.
To perform the trick stand in the centre of the stage
well to the rear with your left side towards the
audience, and contrive to have behind you some
dark background, such as curtains, etc., against
which the thread will be invisible. Taking the ball
in the left hand place it very carefully on the cue,
which you hold at arm's length. Of course you do
not balance it successfully first time but make
several ineffectual attempts ; it is well therefore
to introduce plenty of by-play to heighten the
seeming difficulty. A cough is an excellent oppor-
tunity to let the ball drop. Eventually, however, you
succeed in balancing the ball on the cue, the black
thread being looped over the thumb forms a kind
of railway which not only allows of the ball being
balanced but by this means actually rolled along
the edge of the cue. Of course you must only roll
the ball very slowly or you will possibly give away
the secret of the trick and further only roll the ball

along the cue and back again once ; do not repeat
or you are almost certain to be discovered. When
you have finished take off the ball, lean the cue
against the curtains at the back and step forward
to make your final bow. So ends the juggling act.
This performance can be lengthened or shortened
at will ; any of the small tricks can be omitted or
others added, but the act should always end with
the best trick. Finally let me say that the whole
performance will be much improved if accompanied
by lively music played rather softly and not too
quick.

AN ENCORE

IF the performance has been successfully carried out—and there is no earthly reason why it should not be if you have carefully followed my instructions —you are sure to get called and recalled by the enthusiastic audience, and nothing is more natural than for them to expect more; in other words, they will insist upon your giving an encore trick. Now an encore trick, needless to say, must be as good as if not actually better than the trick that has immediately preceded it, a simple trick in this case would have the effect of spoiling the whole act, would " put the beggar on the gentleman " so to speak. Now the trick I am about to suggest is the most ambitious trick that I have as yet described. It will require a little serious practice and the preparation will be a little more elaborate than for the other tricks. Needless to say the trick is not nearly so difficult as it first appears ; in short it is a " fake." Figure 11 illustrates the effect.

Three billiard cues are stood point downwards on a red billiard ball, the ball at first resting on the floor. On the thick ends of the cues is balanced a small triangular table-top and on this table-top is

placed a lamp or vase or in fact any " showy "
article. The ball is now lifted from the ground with
this load and balanced on the chin—a seemingly

marvellous feat of dex-
terity. Now, as I have
just said, this is not
nearly so difficult a feat
as it first appears. I
will proceed to explain.
Really the most dexter-
ous part of the whole
trick is balancing a
fairly heavy article on
the chin and a little
serious practice will be
necessary to bring about
the required " knack."
I know there are many
amateur   performers
who are really expert
at this kind of thing,
but for those who are
not a hint or two is

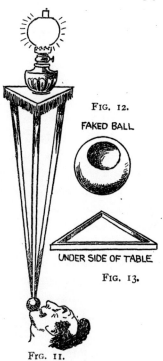

FIG. 12.

FAKED BALL

UNDER SIDE OF TABLE

FIG. 13.

FIG. 11.

absolutely necessary. Practise at first with a broom
or chair, the heavier the article—within reason—
the better and the easier it will be to learn ; it is a
good plan to tie a heavy book, say a Nuttall's
dictionary, to the business end of a long-handled
broom and then practise balancing the other end on

your chin : when you can hold this steady for from
12 to 20 seconds·you may proceed to make prepara-
tions for the trick.

The ball is of wood and is shaped like Figure 12. It
is, of course, painted red, and from a little distance it
looks like a real billiard ball. If you are unable
to make such a ball yourself you will have to purchase one from Hamley's. They cost a shilling.
The table-top you could easily make. It is merely a
triangular piece of wood—two pieces joined would
do ; of course the heavier the wood the easier it will
be to balance. The sides of the triangle should each
measure 15 to 18 inches : round the edge of this you
tack a little beading about an inch wide—timber
merchants sell this kind of beading at about 1½d. per
foot. You may cover this beading if you like with
gold fringe. Figure 13 shows the underside of the
table-top without the fringe. The lamp or vase
that is balanced on the table-top need not be real,
although if you can stand the weight of a real
vase or ornament it would be found much easier
to balance. Theatrical outfitters sell imitation lamps
and vases made of papier mâché : some are of wood.
In this case drive a small nail through the centre
of the table and bore a tiny hole in the underneath
part of the vase and no balancing will be required,
as it could not fall off. In performing the trick
you show the red ball between your finger and
thumb, keeping the hollow part towards you of

course : the ball is kept until required in a small box on your table. You take your stand in the centre of the stage and, placing the ball carefully on the floor, you now appear to stand the points of the cues on the surface of the ball, but in reality you place them in the hollow. You next rest the table-top on the thick end of the cues ; the beading round the edge holding them in position : you now stand the lamp, vase, statuette or whatever it may be, on the table and still holding one of the cues with the left hand you very carefully—some acting here —lift the ball from the floor with the right hand. In lifting it up to your chin you will, of course, have to leave go your hold on the cue with your left hand and put both hands to the ball. I know this sounds a most difficult feat, but try it and you will be surprised how easily it is performed. It is advisable to dab a little powdered rosin on the chin before you walk on the stage to perform this trick. Have the vase and table-top on the table at the start of the performance : never in a juggling show bring on an article from the side of the stage. There is an extremely effective finale to this trick, but it will require a little extra practice; it is, however, well worth the trouble, and has the real professional touch and should therefore appeal strongly to the ambitious amateur.

You are standing in the centre of the stage and well back from the footlights, towards the end of

the applause which is sure to greet this trick,
instead of gently lowering the ball and its load, with
a sudden jerk of the chin, throw the whole lot in the
air, taking one step backwards you catch the lamp
or vase in the right hand as it descends, leaving
the ball, cues and table-top to fall to the ground.
Then quickly recover the ball and make your
bow.

I will now proceed to describe one more trick that
is also very suitable for an encore. This is the well-
known feat of balancing three billiard balls on the
tip of a cue. Quite needless to say, in this case also
it is a " fake." As this is really a most simple trick
to perform—as described below—many of you may
choose it in favour of the preceding one. This
trick, like most other " fakes," requires plenty of
acting and " swank " to carry it off successfully :
in fact I may say at the outset that it would fail
completely as a " straight " juggling feat if not well
acted. You will have to purchase from Hamley's or
some similar firm a cue specially made for the purpose
of performing this trick : this cue is provided with
a very fine needle which runs almost from end to
end of the cue inside. This needle is worked from
the thick end by a small trigger-like catch. The
three balls required are all prepared and you can
either prepare these yourself or buy them. In the
first place they need only be of wood and painted
red, although they are made in both wood and ivory.

Two of the balls have to be drilled right through, the hole must be very fine and, of course, quite straight, the third ball is loaded and Figure 14 explains it. If a wooden ball, saw off about a third of it and replace this portion with lead, the whole is then painted, and if nicely done will completely baffle detection.

FIG. 14.

To perform this trick take your stand in the middle of the stage and holding the cue in your right hand proceed to carefully balance one of the pierced balls on the tip of the cue. Now on no account balance the ball first time; put in plenty of by-play to heighten the apparent difficulty or the effect of the whole trick will be lost. At last you get it to stay on the tip of the cue, you in reality merely with the right thumb push up the trigger catch very slowly which holds the ball in position. Taking the other pierced ball from your pocket you endeavour to balance this on the top of the first ball, and after some more acting succeed in so doing. This is effected by pushing up the catch a little further. You now take the third, i.e. the loaded ball from your pocket and try to balance this on top of the other two. After one or two ineffectual attempts the loaded ball drops to the ground, keeping your eyes on the other two you slowly and carefully stoop to recover the third ball: before you are able to do so, however, you quickly lower the catch, thus causing the two balls to fall to the ground. You now start over again and this time you succeed in balancing all three. Keep them thus for from six to twelve seconds, not longer or the deception will be suspected if not actually discovered ; then carefully remove them one by one, lay the cue on the table and come forward to make your bow.

Of course, should you decide to omit the comedy part of the performance altogether it is quite possible to give quite a neat and creditable little "straight" juggling act by introducing only the serious tricks. However, I for many reasons strongly recommend the comedy act. We are told that the straight juggling show, like the straight acrobatic show, is dead, and I believe it.

I would not, however, advise you to include any comic talk or " patter " in a show of this kind, as unless most skilfully done it would be sure to end in failure, in other words the " bird." Patter is all very fine alone, even for an amateur, but unless you are an experienced performer you are not likely to be able to blend it successfully with juggling.

Printed in Great Britain at
The Mayflower Press, Plymouth. William Brendon & Son, Ltd.

CPSIA information can be obtained at www.ICGtesting.com
Printed in the USA
LVOW061531120612

285781LV00004B/75/A